Lingo Dingo
and the
astronaut
who spoke Spanish

Written by Mark Pallis
Illustrated by James Cottell

For my awesome sons - MP

For Sophia - JC

LINGO DINGO AND THE ASTRONAUT WHO SPOKE SPANISH

All rights reserved. This book or any portion thereof may not be reproduced or used in any manner whatsoever without the express written permission of the publisher except for the use of brief excerpts in a review.

Story edited by Natascha Biebow, Blue Elephant Storyshaping
First Printing, 2023
ISBN: 978-1-915337-43-6
markpallis.com

Lingo Dingo
and the
astronaut
who spoke Spanish

Written by Mark Pallis
Illustrated by James Cottell

NEU WESTEND PRESS

This is Lingo. She's a Dingo and she loves helping.
Anyone. Anytime. Anyhow.

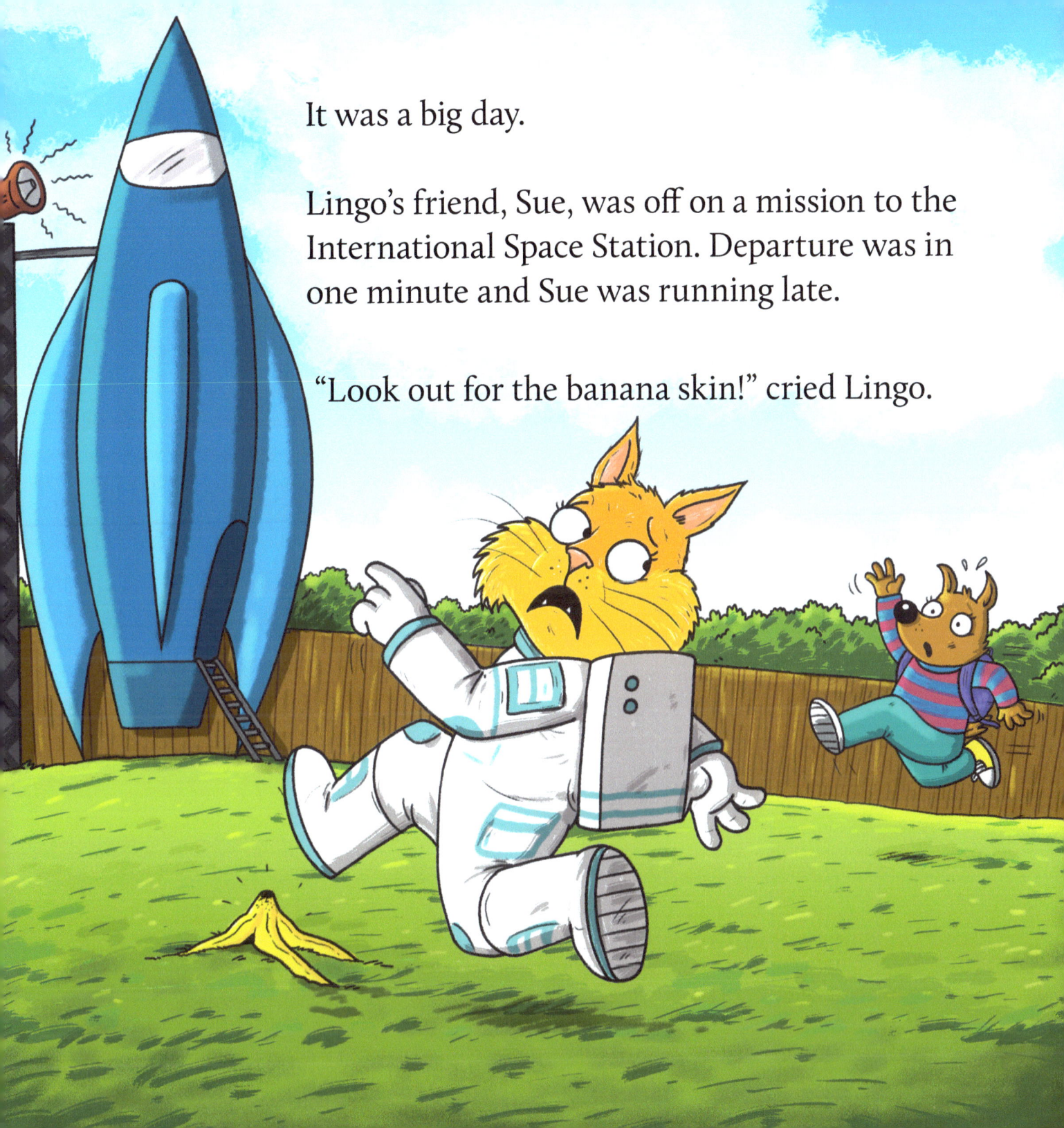

It was a big day.

Lingo's friend, Sue, was off on a mission to the International Space Station. Departure was in one minute and Sue was running late.

"Look out for the banana skin!" cried Lingo.

"I'll be OK, but the mission is over," said Sue.

"I can help!" said Lingo.

But there were only thirty seconds to launch: hurry Lingo!

Quick as a shooting star, Lingo climbed up into the rocket.

"Don't forget this. It's a battery for the Space Station," said Sue.

The countdown began: Five, four...

Lingo soon arrived at the International Space Station.

She was in space and she could f l o a t !

"¡Bienvenida!" said an astronaut. "Me llamo Rex. Soy astronauta."
Lingo tried a reply in Spanish, "Me llamo Lingo."

Bienvenida = Welcome; **Me llamo** = My name is
Soy astronauta = I am an astronaut

Suddenly a BEEPING blared out!
"¿Tienes la batería nueva?" asked Rex.
Lingo wasn't sure what 'batería' meant. She checked her pockets.

¿Tienes la batería nueva? = have you got the new battery?
batería = battery; **nueva/neuvo** = new

"Gírala a la izquierda," said Rex, pointing to the handle.

Lingo turned it right. "¡Derecha no, izquierda!" cried Rex. Lingo turned it left and the hatch swung open.

derecha = right; **izquierda** = left
derecha no, izquierda = not right, left; **gírala a la izquierda** = turn it to the left

Space was waiting for them!
They got straight to work changing the battery.
"Pásame el destornillador, por favor," said Rex.

Lingo passed Rex the screwdriver and he screwed the new battery into place.

el destornillador = the screwdriver; **por favor** = please
Pásame el destornillador = pass me the screwdriver

"¡Todo un éxito!

    Choca los cinco," he said.

Lingo realised Rex wanted a high five.

    Success!

"We did it!"

"Yahoo!"

todo un éxito = we did it
choca los cinco = give me five

The view was incredible.

Rex pointed out all the things to see.

"El sol."

"La tierra."

La tierra = the earth
el sol = the sun

"La luna."

"Las estrellas."

"El brazo robótico."

But Lingo spotted something else ...!

las estrellas = the stars; **la luna** = the moon
el brazo robótico = the robotic arm

"¡Mi osito de peluche!" cried Rex.
Rex's teddy must have floated out of the airlock.
"Usa el brazo robótico," he said.

Lingo was going to use the robotic arm.

mi osito de peluche = my teddy
usa el brazo robótico = use the robotic arm

Rex called out the directions: "Arriba. Abajo. Casi. ¡Cógelo!"

Lingo closed the hand... but Teddy was too far away!

"¡No! Mi osito de peluche está perdido," cried Rex.

"I can help," said Lingo.

She noticed something else floating nearby.

arriba = up; abajo = down; casi = almost; cógelo = grab it;
perdido = lost; mi osito de peluche está perdido = my teddybear is lost

Rex pressed a button and funky music boomed out.

Time to bust some zero gravity dance moves.

"Yo bailo, tú bailas, el osito de peluche baila, nosotros bailamos," laughed Rex.

yo bailo = I dance; **tú bailas** = you dance
Osito baila = teddy dances; **nosotros bailamos** = we dance

"Patata!" said Rex, and took a photo.

Patata = Potato (Say cheese)

"¿Tienes sed?" asked Rex. He squeezed big blobs of water over to Lingo. "Es agua," he said. "¿Tienes hambre?" asked Rex.

¿tienes sed? = are you thirsty?
es agua = that is water; **¿tienes hambre?** = are you hungry?

Lingo and Rex snuggled into bed. What an incredible day.

"Me encanta el Espacio," said Rex.
"Yes," agreed Lingo. "A mí también."
"Duerme bien, Lingo" said Rex.

me encanta = I love; **el Espacio** = space

Lingo didn't have time to wonder what 'duerme bien' meant, she was already fast asleep.

duerme bien = sleep well

Learning to love languages

An additional language opens a child's mind, broadens their horizons and enriches their emotional life. Research has shown that the time between a child's birth and their sixth or seventh birthday is a "golden period" when they are most receptive to new languages. This is because they have an in-built ability to distinguish the sounds they hear and make sense of them. The Story-powered Language Learning Method taps into these natural abilities.

How the Story-powered language learning method works

We create an emotionally engaging and funny story for children and adults to enjoy together, just like any other picture book. Studies show that social interaction, like enjoying a book together, is critical in language learning.

Through the story, we introduce a relatable character who speaks only in the new language. This helps build empathy and a positive attitude towards people who speak different languages. These are both important aspects in laying the foundations for lasting language acquisition in a child's life.

As the story progresses, the child naturally works with the characters to discover the meanings of a wide range of fun new words. Strategic use of humour ensures that this subconscious learning is rewarded with laughter; the child feels good and the first seeds of a lifelong love of languages are sown.

For more information and free learning resources visit www.markpallis.com

You can learn more words and phrases with these hilarious, heartwarming stories from **NEU WESTEND PRESS**

Also available in more than 50 languages, including Spanish-English!

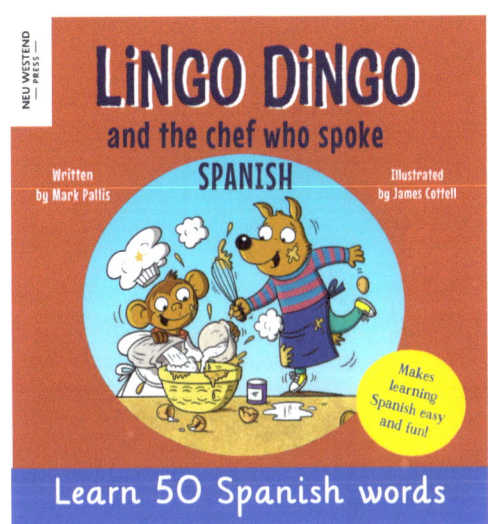
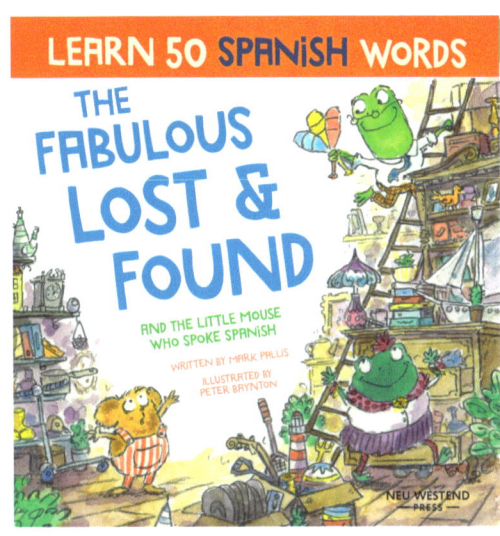

@MARK_PALLIS on twitter
www.markpallis.com

To download your FREE certifcate, and more cool stuff, visit
www.markpallis.com

@jamescottell on INSTAGRAM
www.jamescottellstudios.com

"I want people to be so busy laughing, they don't realise they're learning!"

Mark Pallis

Crab and Whale is the bestselling story of how a little Crab helps a big Whale. It's carefully designed to help even the most energetic children find a moment of calm and focus. It also includes a special mindful breathing exercise and affirmation for children. Also available in Spanish as 'Cangrejo y Ballena.'

Featured as one of Mindful.org's 'Seven Mindful Children's books'

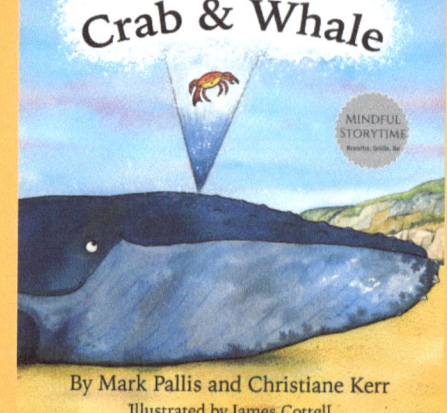

Do you call them hugs or cuddles?

In this funny, heartwarming story, you will laugh out loud as two loveable gibbons try to figure out if a hug is better than a cuddle and, in the process, learn how to get along.

A perfect story for anyone who loves a hug (or a cuddle!)

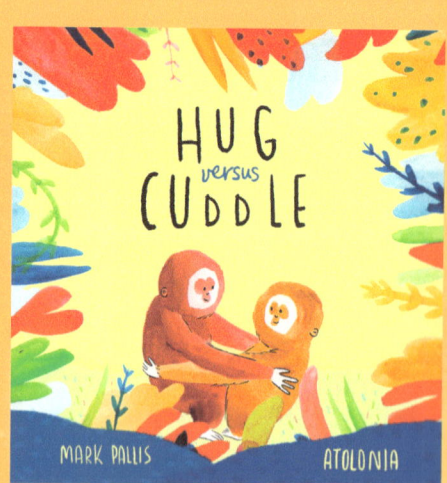

www.markpallis.com

www.ingramcontent.com/pod-product-compliance
Lightning Source LLC
Chambersburg PA
CBHW040021130526
44590CB00036B/49